Mustard

Mustard

MAKING YOUR OWN
GOURMET MUSTARDS

BY JANET HAZEN
ILLUSTRATED BY WARD SCHUMAKER

CHRONICLE BOOKS
SAN FRANCISCO

Library of Congress Cataloging-in-Publication Data
Hazen, Janet.
    Mustard : making your own gourmet mustards / by Janet Hazen ; illustrated
by Ward Schumaker.
      p.   cm.
    ISBN 0-8118-0173-X
    1. Cookery (Mustard)   2. Mustard (Condiment) I. Title.
TX819.M87H39   1993
641.6′384 — dc20   92-23274
                                                        CIP

Book design by Gretchen Scoble.

Printed in Hong Kong.

Distributed in Canada by Raincoast Books, 112 East Third Ave., Vancouver, B.C. V5T 1C8

10 9 8 7 6 5 4 3 2 1

Chronicle Books
275 Fifth Street
San Francisco, CA 94103

TABLE OF CONTENTS

INTRODUCTION

What would a ballpark frank be without that bright yellow stripe of American mustard? And what about the classic combination of warm pastrami on rye, slathered with mustard? Chinese egg rolls seem to beg for a dab of the sinus-clearing concoction, and most wouldn't consider a ham and cheese sandwich complete without a smear of their favorite mustard. We may take mustard for granted—almost everyone has one or two jars of the stuff in the refrigerator—but in fact, mustards can be prepared in a palate-staggering array of flavors; sweet and sour, herbed and spiced, mild and hot. Nearly every culture has developed at least one unique version of mustard.

The English word *mustard* comes from the Latin *mustum ardens,* which translates to "burning must." The Romans may have made the first prepared mustards by combining fermented grape juice (must) with mustard seeds to form a spreadable paste. The mustards we make today come from the seeds of three species of plants from the Cruciferae family: black mustard *(Brassica nigra),* brown mustard *(Brassica juncea),* and yellow mustard *(Sinapis alba).* The near and distant culinary relatives of mustard in the Cruciferae family include Brussel sprouts, cauliflower, kale, cabbage, turnips, and watercress.

Black, brown, and yellow mustard plants are annuals, and all produce small yellow flowers. The black mustard plant, when left to its own devices, can grow to 10 or 12 feet in height, but the tamer brown and yellow plants generally grow to approximately 2½ to 3 feet tall. All produce seeds; the black mustard plant produces the smallest seeds, the brown seeds are larger than the black, and the yellow seeds are just a bit larger still. The seeds are harvested in late summer, when they are fully developed and ready to burst; they are then left to dry. After drying, the seeds are threshed and packaged. Ironically, the size of the seed relates to the intensity of flavor in reverse order—the smaller the seed, the bigger the flavor. Yellow mustard seeds are the mildest in flavor, brown seeds are considerably more flavorful than yellow, and black seeds are the most pungent of all.

Black mustard originated in the Middle East and the temperate zones of Asia, but it is now grown primarily in southern Italy, India, and Ethiopia. Because the plant grows to such a large size, it can be unruly and problematic for farmers. Black mustard seeds must be harvested by hand, and for this reason, and many others, it is the least popular type of mustard for commercial growers.

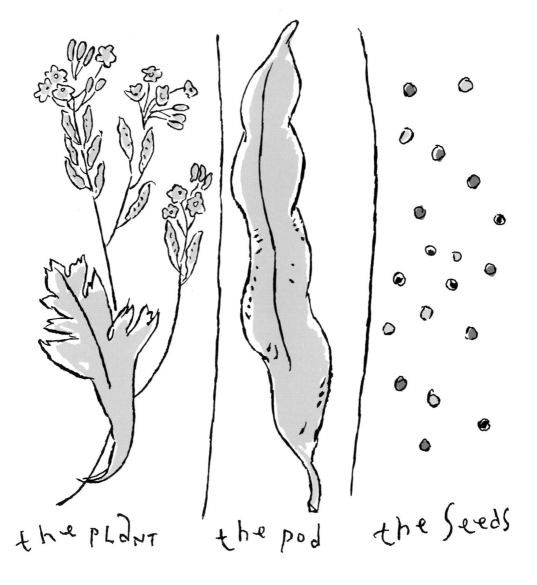

the plant   the pod   the seeds

Brown mustard is native to India, but it is now grown widely in parts of China, England, northern Europe, and Canada. The plant is smaller and easier to control than the black mustard plants, and is favored by most mustard growers worldwide. Yellow mustard is native to the Mediterranean, but is also grown with great success in England, the United States, and Canada. The plants that produce yellow and brown seeds are neat and tidy, and the seeds are easily harvested by machine.

Mustard seeds were first utilized in ancient cuisines to camouflage the rank flavors of stale meat and to add zest to what would have been a bland and boring diet. Records show that communities in India and Sumeria used mustard seeds and mustard oil as early as 3000 B.C., and it is believed that mustard was used for culinary purposes around 1500 B.C. in parts of Asia. The basic diet of this time consisted of barley, wheat, and a variety of meats, which were flavored with sesame oil and often seasoned with mustard seeds. Ancient Greeks treated mustard with the greatest respect and regarded it as a fundamental cooking ingredient as well as a magical drug. It was the Romans, however, who turned mustard seeds into a versatile paste by combining it with grape must, vinegar, oil, and honey. They used it to flavor and complement meats and vegetables and for pickling a wide range of fresh foods. The magical seeds were considered a preservative as well as an indispensable flavoring agent, and they were also used as a cure-all for many physical ailments.

It is believed the Romans introduced mustard seeds to the French in the tenth century A.D. The monks of St. Germain des Pres in Paris gleaned as much information about mustard from the Romans as possible and eventually began producing mustard according to their own recipes. By the thirteenth century, Dijon was recognized as a center for mustard making, and during the 1400s, laws were introduced to regulate and standardize production. In 1937, Dijon mustard gained its own *Appellation Contrôllée d'Origine,* meaning "controlled name of origin," and today, Dijon is considered the mustard capital of the world.

Although mustard grew wild in England, it wasn't until the arrival of the Romans in the later part of the tenth century that mustard making became popular. In England during the Middle Ages, mustards were used to cover the pungent flavors of meat and smoked fish, and by the thirteenth century, authorized mustard makers produced large quantities of the condiment for sale to the public.

In America, Indians dried the seeds of mustard plants and used them to flavor their foods, but it was Irish, English, German, and Scandinavian immigrants who introduced the pastes to early American settlers. The arrival of mustard was advertised in 1735 in the South Carolina *Gazette:* "Just imported from London by John Watson . . . mustard seed." Mustard was used in sausage recipes, baked beans, sauces, soups, and stews, and was served with roasted meats and smoked fish.

The use of mustard for medicinal purposes dates back to ancient Greeks and Romans, who mixed it with vinegar to make a paste suitable for rubbing onto the skin. They also took the seeds internally to help treat a variety of physical maladies. It was the British herbalists of the sixteenth and seventeenth centuries, however, who exploited the medicinal uses of mustard to the fullest. John Gerard, in his *Herbal* of 1597, stated that "the seede of Mustarde pounded with vinegar is an excellent sauce, good to be eaten with any grosse meates, either fish or flesh, because it doth help digestion, warmeth the stomache and provoketh appetite." Mustard was also given to those with bad circulation, heart and lung problems, fevers, or the flu. It was often applied as a plaster, usually to the chest area, where difficult breathing was most evident. Mustard was also given to those with toothaches, sore throats, neck and back pain, and rheumatism. Nicholas Culpeper, author of *The Complete Herbal* (1653), claimed mustard was a good antidote against snake poison and poisonous mushrooms. The producers of Colman's mustard noted the health benefits of their product in a nineteenth-century advertising campaign: "It purges the body of toxic products, relieving pain, giving a feeling of warmth and well-being, and an increased flow of blood; it stimulates capillary circulation, relieves rheumatism, colds, flu, bronchitis, coughs on the chest, aches in the nape of the neck, neuralgia in the side of the face, and toothache." Today, mustard is still used therapeutically, primarily in mustard plasters and in herbal remedies.

As a condiment and in cooking, mustard has far-reaching appeal and diverse uses. The flavor of mustard can be discreet and subtle or assertive and primary. It complements foods and illuminates the natural flavors of many dishes, but it can also star as the principal taste in many prepared foods. It is used in numerous dishes as a thickening and flavoring agent and as a preservative. Mustard is used in the commercial preparation of sausages and bologna, soups, pickles, mayonnaise, salad dressings and vinaigrettes, sauces, relishes, and marinades.

The seeds of the plant, as well as prepared pastes, are used in the cuisines of India, the Mediterranean, the Caribbean, northern Europe, the Balkan States, Asia, the United States, and Africa. Almost every country has a special use for mustard in one form or another. The Chinese mix water or vinegar with an incendiary yellow mustard powder and serve the paste with deep-fried foods such as egg rolls. In India, the seeds are favored in a great number of dishes: chutneys, pickles, curries, stews, and soups, and in meat, poultry, fish, and vegetable dishes. The seeds are often toasted in a pan over low heat, or mixed with other spices and cooked in a small amount of *ghee* (clarified butter).

Northern Europeans are fond of spreading a variety of prepared mustards onto breads and forming them into interesting sandwiches. Likewise, mustards are served with all sorts of cured, salted, and smoked meats and sausages throughout Europe. In France, prepared mustard is put to use in countless ways — in vinaigrettes and aioli, soups and stews, *ragoûts* and *daubes,* as well as straight from the jar, spread onto bread and accompanied by cheese and sliced meats. In America we tend to think of mustard as the perfect condiment for hot dogs and hamburgers, but those in the know also use mustard when preparing vinaigrettes, salad dressings, potato salad, coleslaw, bean dishes, and hundreds of other hot and cold dishes.

The heat in mustard comes from the enzyme
myrosin, which is released when the seed is crushed or
bruised and mixed with a liquid.

Americans are now focusing on homemade, unadulterated, and preservative-free foods, so it's only natural that we turn to making mustards at home. There is a much broader range of mustard flavors accessible to home cooks who choose to make their own mustards. There are many unusual commercial mustards available, but the freedom to create a particular style of mustard at home is a great advantage. Preparing these inviting, unique, and original pastes requires a spice or coffee grinder, a few bowls, and only a few standard ingredients. It literally takes just minutes to put together a fine mustard, and after a couple of weeks of curing time in the refrigerator, you will have a wonderful, flavorful, and robust condiment to use in cooking, or simply straight from the jar. Mustard also serves as a low-fat, low-calorie flavoring agent that easily finds its way into a wide assortment of recipes.

The following recipes are just a sampling of the unique mustards that can be made with various combinations of yellow and brown mustard seeds, vinegars, wine, champagne, beer, and a variety of herbs, spices, and flavoring agents. One word of caution: these mustards may be much hotter and more intensely flavored than the commercial brands you are used to. Some of them are truly sinus clearing, while others are concentrated in flavor but not painfully strong. Surprisingly, the recipes that include other "heating" elements, such as black pepper, fresh chilies, or dried red chilies, are milder than the recipes that depend solely on mustard seeds for their heat.

The first part of this book contains eighteen original recipes for making homemade mustards. The second part is devoted to recipes for making condiments, sauces, marinades, and dressings, many of which provide delightful ways of using your homemade mustards. Let these formulas for mustard act as a springboard for your creative abilities in the kitchen—have some fun concocting your own mustards and experimenting with them in your cooking.

*To boost the flavor of soups, stews,
or ragoûts made with meat, poultry, or dried
legumes, add 2 tablespoons of any variety
of mustard during the last 20 minutes of cooking.
The mustard acts as a natural thickener,
adds flavor, and enhances the flavors of the
meat, poultry, or beans.*

MAKING HOMEMADE MUSTARD

There aren't any tricks or complicated steps to making mustard in your own kitchen. Whole, partially ground, finely ground, or powdered mustard seeds are the main ingredients needed for making mustard. Whole brown seeds are more assertive in flavor than the yellow, and the black are the most biting of all. Any of the seeds can be used to make the pastes, but yellow, or a combination of yellow and brown, are commonly utilized for making most mustards. Powdered mustard is also used to make mustard, but it's nice to have both the whole yellow and brown seeds in addition to the powder when you make homemade mustards — the seeds add a pleasing texture and flavor.

Although whole yellow mustard seeds can be the mildest of all the seeds, mustards made entirely from their powder (rather than a combination of partially ground seeds and powder) are extremely pungent. Because of this, these types of mustards usually need to be softened with sugar, honey, or other flavoring agents.

There are only two main guidelines to follow when making mustard: use cold water or cold liquids, and cure the mustard in the refrigerator for at least one week before using. Boiling water, when combined with mustard, kills the myrosin enzyme and leaves the mustard full of unconverted glucoside, making the mustard extremely unpleasant and bitter. Curing helps the flavors marry, allows time for the mustard to mellow, and helps to reduce the sharp flavor initially present in many homemade mustards.

A fine, balanced, and full-flavored mustard consists of several components. Mustard seeds form the backbone of the paste, but a strong-flavored liquid is necessary not only for making the seeds into a spreadable paste, but also for activating the enzyme that gives mustard its characteristic punch. Adding water alone would make a pretty boring mustard, so most recipes incorporate vinegars, wine, beer, or citrus juices to add interest. If vinegar is the primary liquid used in a recipe, it may be necessary to balance the acidity with some kind of sweetening agent such as honey, molasses, brown or white sugar, maple syrup, or corn syrup.

Certain fruits and vegetables can also be added to mustard pastes, particularly citrus fruits, hot and sweet peppers, tomatoes, onions, and garlic. These fresh ingredients lend texture, color, and flavor and also help to soften the frequently sharp flavor of pure mustard. In addition to sweet and tart flavors, we want to consider the accents—the herbs and spices or other flavors used to give a definite character to the mustard. Any combination of these basic ingredients yields an excellent mustard suitable for using straight from the jar as a condiment, or for adding to soups, stews, salads, vinaigrettes, or sauces.

PURCHASING THE RAW MATERIALS: MUSTARD POWDER AND SEEDS

Mustard is available in two forms: ground powder and whole seeds. Ground mustard, also known as mustard flour or mustard powder, is sold in tins or in bulk and is possibly the most popular form of mustard used for cooking. Yellow and brown mustard seeds are readily available in natural food stores; spice and herb shops; ethnic markets that sell East Indian, Southeast Asian, Italian, or Middle Eastern foods; and in some gourmet food stores.

When purchasing mustard powder, I recommend buying it in a tin rather than bulk. It's difficult to determine how long a bulk jar of mustard powder has been sitting on the shelf and, like all spices, once ground it loses some of its strength and character. Chances are, ground mustard sold in tightly closed tins (such as the 4-ounce boxes of Colman's Mustard) is fresher.

Mustard seeds stored at cool room temperature can last up to one year and can therefore be safely purchased in bulk. Yellow and brown seeds are more prevalent than black seeds, but most East Indian food stores and some specialty food shops and natural food stores also stock the black seeds. In any event, brown seeds can be used in place of black seeds for most purposes, and the recipes in this book use only yellow and brown seeds. It is not advisable to substitute yellow seeds for brown seeds because their flavors are quite distinct.

STORING MUSTARD

Mustard powder can be stored in a tightly sealed container in a cool, dark place for several months. Mustard seeds can be stored in a tightly sealed plastic bag or in a glass jar or container with a tight-fitting lid at room temperature for up to one year. Unopened jars of tightly sealed commercial prepared mustard can be stored at room temperature for years, but once opened, they should be refrigerated. The mustards in this book do not contain any artificial preservatives, so always store these homemade mustards in a tightly covered container in the refrigerator.

Unlike store-bought prepared mustards, most homemade mustards need a short "curing" period of approximately one to three weeks in an airtight container in the refrigerator before they are ready to eat. After this time they can be used as a condiment or in cooking. However, when using homemade mustards from the first portion of this book to make the recipes for condiments, sauces, marinades, and dressings in the second portion, it isn't crucial to cure the mustards first. A cured mustard will produce a milder, smoother, more homogenized flavor, but since the mustards are combined with many other ingredients in the recipes, the subtleties of the homemade mustard aren't as obvious as if they were being eaten alone.

Unless otherwise noted, the homemade mustards in this book can be used for up to one year. However, both store-bought and homemade prepared mustards lose their pungency and power with time. Jars that have been opened, recapped, and stored in the refrigerator for longer than six months will invariably be flat tasting and bland, and mustards held over one year can be discarded.

PREPARING MUSTARD POWDER AND SEEDS

Mustard powder requires no preparation before using it in cooked dishes or before using it to make prepared mustard. If the mustard has dried a bit and has formed little chunks, simply place it in a small bowl and crush the chunks with the back of a spoon.

Mustard seeds are used whole, partially ground, or finely ground, in cooked dishes or for making prepared mustard. To crush mustard seeds, place them in a mortar and crush with the pestle until the desired consistency is achieved. Alternatively, place them in an electric spice or coffee grinder and grind to the desired coarseness. In a pinch, a high-power blender can be used to crush the seeds, but I recommend a spice or coffee grinder for the best results. Yellow seeds, if ground as finely as possible and strained through a fine sieve, are a good substitute for commercial mustard powder. Yellow seeds are the softest, brown seeds are semisoft, and the black seeds are harder still. For this reason, it's best to grind each type of seed separately.

COOKING WITH MUSTARD

Mustard powder, mustard seeds, and prepared mustards can all be used for cooking. Depending on the texture and intensity of flavor desired, whole, medium-ground, or finely ground seeds may be added to a dish. Prepared mustard and finely ground seeds impart the most flavor but have little texture; coarsely ground seeds yield a moderate amount of both flavor and texture. Whole seeds are the most innocuous when it comes to flavor, but they add the most texture. When a very smooth consistency is desired, it's best to add prepared mustards made with finely ground seeds, or use mustard powder or finely ground mustard seeds strained through a fine wire sieve.

Prepared mustard and finely ground seeds are a natural thickening agent; for this reason mustard is often used for making dressings, mayonnaise, vinaigrettes, and sauces. Bear this in mind when adding to prepared dishes. Prepared commercial and homemade mustards tend to thicken as they sit, so when using a mustard that has been refrigerated for a while, you may have to thin it with a little water, vinegar, wine, or other suitable liquid before using it in cooking or as a condiment.

Like many herbs, spices, and flavoring agents, the flavor and intensity of mustard lessens as it cooks, so if a very pronounced flavor is desired, add the mustard paste, finely ground seeds, or powder toward the end of the cooking time. Whole seeds are not greatly affected by heat, and are therefore generally added to foods at the beginning of cooking.

Honey mustard or any prepared mustard with a large percentage of sugar may caramelize as it cooks. For example, if you rub honey mustard on the skin of meat or poultry before grilling or roasting at high temperatures, the skin may burn well before the interior is cooked. To prevent this from happening, choose a mustard with less sugar, cook slowly at a lower temperature, or cover the food with foil when the skin starts to brown.

MUSTARD RECIPES

MAPLE–APPLE CIDER MUSTARD

Slightly sweet and coarse-textured, this delightful mustard has a very subtle maple flavor and is excellent served as a condiment with baked ham or roast pork. Alternatively, spread a thin layer of the mustard on the meat during the last 10 minutes of cooking for a light glazed effect and subtle mustard flavor.

Makes about 1 cup.

¼ cup whole yellow mustard seeds, coarsely ground
¼ cup whole brown mustard seeds, coarsely ground
¼ cup mustard powder
½ cup water
3 tablespoons apple cider vinegar
3 tablespoons pure maple syrup
1 teaspoon salt
½ teaspoon pepper

Place the mustard seeds and powder in a medium bowl; mix well. Add the water, vinegar, maple syrup, salt, and pepper and mix well to form a paste. Transfer to a clean, dry jar or bowl, cover tightly, and refrigerate for 2 weeks before using.

Hazelnut Mustard

This fine mustard, laced with chopped hazelnuts and hazelnut oil, is rich, nutty, and excellent served as a condiment with red meats, pork, and duck. Use a bit of this mustard when making vinaigrettes, or add to beef stew or duck ragoût for a nutty mustard flavor. A good-quality imported hazelnut oil gives the mustard a fine texture and bold hazelnut flavor, but if you can't find hazelnut oil, use a good-quality extra-virgin olive oil.

Makes about ¾ cup.

14 toasted hazelnuts, skins removed, coarsely chopped
½ cup whole yellow mustard seeds, coarsely ground
½ cup water

3 tablespoons balsamic vinegar
¼ cup hazelnut oil
1 teaspoon salt
½ teaspoon pepper

Place all of the ingredients in a blender. Purée until fairly smooth and thoroughly mixed, frequently scraping the sides of the container. Transfer to a clean, dry jar or bowl, cover tightly, and refrigerate for 2 weeks before using.

TARRAGON MUSTARD

Traditionally used in sauces for roast chicken, this mustard may be used with any kind of poultry or as a sandwich spread. Rub on roasted chicken breasts just before serving, or combine with sour cream to make a light sauce for poached chicken breasts or fish. To enliven chicken salads, add a couple of spoonfuls of this mustard to the mayonnaise.

Makes about 1 cup.

¼ cup whole yellow mustard seeds, finely ground
¼ cup mustard powder
¼ cup champagne vinegar or white wine vinegar
½ cup water

1 tablespoon light brown sugar
1½ tablespoons dried tarragon or 3 tablespoons minced fresh tarragon
1 clove garlic, minced
1 teaspoon salt

In a medium bowl, combine the mustard seeds, mustard powder, champagne vinegar, and water; mix well. Add the sugar, tarragon, garlic, and salt and mix well to form a smooth paste. Transfer to a clean, dry jar or bowl, cover tightly, and refrigerate for 2 weeks before using.

tarragon

BRITISH BEER MUSTARD

Choose a robust imported amber ale or stout for this spiced mustard. Excellent for adding to hearty meat stews, soups, or ragoûts, this coarse-grained dark mustard is strong and assertive and also pairs well with dark bread, smoked sausages, and very strong cheeses.

Makes about 1 1/2 cups.

3/4 cup whole brown mustard seeds, coarsely ground
1/4 cup mustard powder
4 allspice berries, finely ground
2 teaspoons each ground coriander and turmeric
1/2 teaspoon celery seeds
1 cup British amber ale or stout (Guinness)
2 cloves garlic, minced
1 teaspoon salt

Place all of the ingredients in a blender. Purée until fairly smooth and thoroughly mixed, frequently scraping the sides of the container. Transfer to a clean, dry jar or bowl, cover tightly, and refrigerate for 2 weeks before using.

FIVE-SPICE BROWN MUSTARD

Spicy and sweet, this dark brown mustard is delicious served with strong German or Danish cheeses, smoked ham, and fish, or combined with a little beer and used as a basting medium for baked ham or pork.

Makes about 1 cup.

¾ cup whole brown mustard seeds, coarsely ground
5 allspice berries, finely ground
1 teaspoon each ground coriander and caraway seeds
5 whole cloves, finely ground
3 tablespoons dark brown sugar
⅓ cup water
¼ cup champagne vinegar or white wine vinegar
2 tablespoons olive oil
1 teaspoon salt

Place the mustard seeds in a medium bowl. Combine the spices in a small bowl; mix well. Sift the spices into the mustard seeds using a fine wire mesh or strainer. Add the sugar and mix well. Add the water, vinegar, olive oil, and salt; mix well until combined. Transfer to a clean, dry jar or bowl, cover tightly, and refrigerate for 2 weeks before using.

Brown Sugar–Sherry Mustard

Slightly sweet, hot, and smooth in texture, this mustard is ideal for using in marinades, sauces, and vinaigrettes and for pairing with smoked meats. Add a couple of spoonfuls to a pot of beans or chicken salad, or spread it on baked ham during the last 10 minutes of cooking.

Makes about ¾ cup.

½ cup mustard powder
4 tablespoons sherry wine
3 tablespoons sherry vinegar
¼ cup firmly packed dark brown sugar
1 clove garlic, minced
1 teaspoon salt
½ teaspoon pepper

Place the mustard powder in a small bowl. Add the sherry wine and the vinegar and mix to form a paste. Add the sugar, garlic, salt, and pepper; mix well. Transfer to a clean, dry jar or bowl, cover tightly, and refrigerate for 2 weeks before using.

HONEY MUSTARD

Although this mustard is made with plenty of honey, it still has quite a bite! Sweet, hot, and smooth in texture, this mustard is delicious with smoked meats or poultry, or spread sparingly on breads to accompany strong cheeses. It also adds zip to commercial marinades and makes a good dipping sauce for deep-fried foods.

Makes about 1¼ cups.

1 cup mustard powder
¼ cup white wine vinegar
¼ cup honey
1 clove garlic, minced
1 teaspoon salt
½ teaspoon white pepper

In a small bowl, combine the mustard powder with the vinegar, honey, and garlic; mix well until smooth. Add the salt and pepper and mix well. Transfer to a clean, dry jar or bowl, cover tightly, and refrigerate for 2 weeks before using.

Hot Chili Coarse-Grained Mustard

Tiny, fiery dried chili peppers add just a touch of heat to this coarse-textured mustard, but they also temper the natural heating qualities of the mustard seeds and powder. This mustard adds zip to cream sauces, salad dressings, stews, soups, and pasta dishes, and it is also good as a sandwich spread.

Makes about 1 cup.

⅓ cup whole yellow mustard seeds, coarsely ground
¼ cup whole brown mustard seeds, coarsely ground
3 tablespoons mustard powder
¼ cup water
¼ cup dry white wine

3 tablespoons white wine vinegar
2 tablespoons light brown sugar
3 tablespoons olive oil
3 small Chinese or Mexican dried hot chili peppers, coarsely ground
1 teaspoon turmeric
1½ teaspoons salt

Place all of the ingredients in a blender. Purée until fairly smooth and well mixed, frequently scraping the sides of the blender. Transfer to a clean, dry jar or bowl, cover tightly, and refrigerate for 2 weeks before using.

HERBED TOMATO MUSTARD

A mild, rose-tinted paste, this tomato-herb mustard adds zest and color to salad dressings and vinaigrettes and is nice blended with mayonnaise and used as a summer vegetable dipping sauce.

Makes about ³/₄ cup.

⅓ cup whole yellow mustard seeds, finely ground
¼ cup red wine vinegar
2 tablespoons water
1 tablespoon olive oil
2 cloves garlic, minced

1 teaspoon each dried basil, oregano, and chervil
1 small tomato, peeled, seeded, and finely chopped (about ½ cup)
1 teaspoon salt
½ teaspoon black pepper

Place all of the ingredients in a blender. Purée until fairly smooth and thoroughly mixed, frequently scraping the sides of the container. Transfer to a clean, dry jar or bowl, cover tightly, and refrigerate for 2 weeks before using.

STRAWBERRY MUSTARD

This fruity pink mustard is excellent spread on bread and served with thin slices of ham and cheese. It might be interesting to add a spoonful to a mayonnaise-based dressing for fruit salad. Because it is made with fresh strawberries, it is more perishable than most mustards. It is best used within a month.

Makes about ¾ cup.

½ cup whole yellow mustard seeds, finely ground
½ cup raspberry vinegar
3 tablespoons water
2 tablespoons vegetable or light olive oil
5 ripe strawberries, stemmed and halved
½ teaspoon finely ground pink peppercorns
1 teaspoon salt

Place all of the ingredients in a blender. Purée until fairly smooth and thoroughly mixed, frequently scraping the sides of the container.
Transfer to a clean, dry jar or bowl, cover tightly, and refrigerate for 1 week before using.

GERMAN-STYLE COARSE-GRAINED MUSTARD

Thick and coarse, this complex mustard incorporates many spices and is excellent spread on hot sausages or ham. It is also a nice accompaniment to smoked meats served with sauerkraut, cooked cabbage, and potatoes. Use this mustard in marinades for meat and poultry and for accenting German-style potato salads.

Makes about 2 cups.

½ cup whole brown mustard seeds, coarsely ground
½ cup whole yellow mustard seeds, coarsely ground
¾ cup dry white wine
½ teaspoon ground caraway seeds
6 allspice berries, finely ground
Pinch each ground mace, cloves, and cinnamon
3 tablespoons olive oil
2 tablespoons Worcestershire sauce
¼ cup malt or balsamic vinegar
2 cloves garlic, minced
1 teaspoon salt

Place all of the ingredients in a blender. Purée until fairly smooth and thoroughly mixed, scraping the sides of the container frequently. Transfer to a clean, dry jar or bowl, cover tightly, and refrigerate for 2 weeks before using.

BLACK PEPPER–GARLIC MUSTARD

Mild in flavor and blond in color, this garlic-infused mustard is excellent spread on bread and served with sliced cured or smoked meats, or spread on a toasted baguette and topped with grilled eggplant and cheese to make an open-faced sandwich. A tablespoon or two also enhances the flavor of meat loaf, beef stews, and macaroni and cheese.

Makes about 1 cup.

6 large unpeeled cloves garlic
2 cups water
¾ cup whole yellow mustard seeds,
   finely ground
⅓ cup water

¼ cup champagne vinegar or
   white wine vinegar
3 tablespoons olive oil
1 tablespoon whole black peppercorns,
   coarsely cracked
1½ teaspoons salt

Place the garlic and water in a small saucepan. Bring to a boil over high heat. Cook for 10 to 12 minutes or until the garlic is very soft. Drain well and remove the skins from the garlic. Place in a blender along with the remaining ingredients. Purée until fairly smooth and well mixed, frequently scraping the sides of the container. Transfer to a clean, dry jar or bowl, cover tightly, and refrigerate for 1 week before using.

CHINESE-STYLE FIRE MUSTARD

True to Chinese-style mustards, this incendiary condiment is sure to please the most dedicated "hothead," but use the paste sparingly for those with a more delicate palate. This smooth-textured mustard is good with deep-fried foods and in marinades for red meats. Combine with milder ingredients such as mayonnaise or sour cream or a combination of low-sodium soy sauce, honey, and rice wine vinegar to make a dipping sauce for Chinese appetizers.

Makes about 1 cup.

1 cup mustard powder
1 teaspoon Szechwan peppercorns, finely ground and sifted
2 star anise, ground
1 teaspoon each ground caraway seeds and cinnamon
⅓ cup water
3 tablespoons seasoned rice wine vinegar
1 tablespoon soy sauce
1 clove garlic, minced

In a medium bowl, combine the mustard powder and spices. Add the water, vinegar, and soy sauce and mix well to form a paste. Add the garlic and mix well. Transfer to a clean, dry jar or bowl, cover tightly, and refrigerate for 2 weeks before using.

JALAPEÑO-CUMIN MUSTARD

Mexican-inspired ingredients make this mustard peppy and unique. Contrary to what you might think, this mustard is milder than many others that do not include fresh chili peppers. Combine ½ cup of the mustard with ¾ cup of peanut or olive oil to make a fine marinade for poultry, pork, or beef, or simply use it straight from the jar for making sandwiches.

Makes about 1 cup.

½ cup mustard powder
½ cup whole yellow mustard seeds
⅓ cup apple cider vinegar
3 tablespoons water
3 tablespoons light brown sugar

2 teaspoons ground cumin
2 jalapeño peppers, stemmed, seeded, and minced
1 clove garlic, minced
1 teaspoon salt

Place all of the ingredients in a blender. Purée until fairly smooth and thoroughly mixed, frequently scraping the sides of the container. Transfer to a clean, dry jar or bowl, cover tightly, and refrigerate for 2 weeks before using.

MOLASSES MUSTARD

This is an ideal mustard to add to baked beans because it contains ingredients often used in the preparation of the classic cold-weather dish. Add about ¼ cup of the mustard to the beans during the last 30 minutes of cooking time. It is also delicious when spread on dark bread and used for steak sandwiches. This mustard would be a fine choice for using in a meat marinade.

Makes about 1 cup.

½ cup whole brown mustard seeds, coarsely ground
1 cup cold water
½ cup mustard powder
3 tablespoons light molasses
1 tablespoon ground coriander
1 clove garlic, minced
2 teaspoons salt

Place the mustard seeds and water in a bowl. Let soak at room temperature for 2 hours. Pour off and discard the water (do not strain). Place the soaked mustard seeds in a medium bowl along with the mustard powder, molasses, coriander, garlic, and salt. Mix well. Transfer to a clean, dry jar or bowl, cover tightly, and refrigerate for 2 weeks before using.

CHAMPAGNE MUSTARD

Smooth and herbaceous, this mustard is excellent with cooked poultry and vegetables. Spread a thin layer on crackers or bread and serve with sliced smoked chicken or turkey and assorted cheeses. This mustard is a good substitute for the classic Dijon mustard.

Makes about 1 cup.

¼ cup whole yellow mustard seeds, finely ground
¾ cup mustard powder
2 tablespoons light brown sugar
¾ cup champagne or sparkling wine
½ teaspoon each dried tarragon, basil, and thyme
1 clove garlic, minced
1 teaspoon salt

In a small bowl, combine the mustard seeds and powder. Add the sugar, champagne, herbs, garlic, and salt; mix well. Transfer to a clean, dry jar or bowl, cover tightly, and refrigerate for 2 weeks before using.

47

GINGER-TERIYAKI MUSTARD

This mustard is exceedingly hot, only barely tempered by the addition of brown sugar and slightly sweet teriyaki sauce. Its fresh taste of ginger makes this ideal for serving with grilled oily fish, such as mackerel or sardines, and when combined with equal parts teriyaki sauce and sweet wine vinegar, it makes a tingling dipping sauce for Asian appetizers.

Makes about 1 cup.

¼ cup whole dark mustard seeds, finely ground
½ cup mustard powder
¼ cup water
2 tablespoons white wine vinegar
3 tablespoons teriyaki sauce
2 tablespoons dark brown sugar
2 cloves garlic, minced
⅓ cup finely minced fresh ginger root

Place the mustard seeds and powder in a medium bowl; mix well. Add the water, vinegar, and teriyaki sauce and mix well to form a paste. Add the sugar, garlic, and ginger and mix well. Transfer to a clean, dry jar or bowl, cover tightly, and refrigerate for 1 week before using.

THREE-CITRUS MUSTARD

Mild, refreshing, and slightly sweet, this mustard can be spread on crackers and topped with sliced cucumbers or smoked fish for a pleasing appetizer. It is also excellent when used in vinaigrettes or when combined with mayonnaise to make a tart dipping sauce for cooked or raw vegetables.

Makes about 1 ¼ cups.

¾ cup mustard powder
½ cup whole yellow mustard seeds
⅓ cup fresh lemon juice
Juice from 1 lime
Juice from 1 orange

3 tablespoons water
2 tablespoons light brown sugar
Zest from 1 orange
½ teaspoon ground nutmeg
½ teaspoon salt

In a small bowl combine the mustard powder and the seeds. Add the lemon juice, lime juice, orange juice, and water; mix to form a paste. Add the sugar, orange zest, nutmeg, and salt; mix well. Transfer to a clean, dry jar or bowl, cover tightly, and refrigerate for 2 weeks before using.

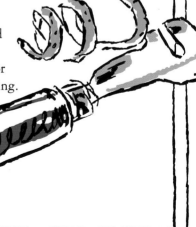

"Mustard" is also known as chiehi
in certain dialects of Chinese, rai *in India,*
mostaza *in Spain,* sanape *in Italy,*
senf *in Germany,* moutarde *in France,*
mosterd *in Holland, and*
biji sawi *in Malaysia.*

Condiments, Sauces, Marinades, and Dressings

APPLE-APRICOT CHUTNEY WITH YELLOW MUSTARD

This mustard-infused, Indian-style chutney is excellent with smoked or cured meats, game, poultry, or even spread onto crackers or bread and paired with strong-flavored cheeses.

Makes about 2 cups.

1 medium onion, cut into small dice
2 medium apples, cored and
   cut into small dice
3 tablespoons peanut oil
3 tablespoons whole brown
   mustard seeds
1 tablespoon turmeric
1 teaspoon each ground mace
   and cardamom
Pinch ground cloves

¾ cup finely chopped dried apricots
1 cup fresh orange juice
1 cup water
2 tablespoons sherry wine vinegar
2 tablespoons Jalapeño-Cumin
   Mustard (page 44), Hot Chili
   Coarse-Grained Mustard
   (page 36), or Brown Sugar–
   Sherry Mustard (page 33)
Salt and pepper, to taste

In a large sauté pan, cook the onion and apples in the peanut oil over moderately high heat for 4 or 5 minutes, stirring frequently. Add the mustard seeds, spices, and apricots and cook over high heat for 2 minutes, stirring constantly. Add the orange juice and water and bring to a boil. Reduce the heat to moderately low and cook for 15 minutes or until the mixture is thick and the liquid has evaporated. Add the vinegar and mustard and mix well. Season with salt and pepper and cool to room temperature. Transfer to a clean, dry jar or bowl and cover tightly. Can be stored in the refrigerator for up to 3 weeks.

SOUR CREAM MUSTARD SAUCE

Spoon this mustard-spiked, creamy sauce over chilled chicken breasts or fish or roasted and cooled pork tenderloin. It also makes an easy sauce for blanched and chilled mixed vegetables and potatoes.

Makes about 1 cup.

¾ cup sour cream
2 tablespoons Champagne Mustard (page 47), Tarragon Mustard (page 29),
    or Dijon mustard
1 tablespoon British Beer Mustard (page 30), or Maple–Apple Cider Mustard
    (page 27)
2 tablespoons minced parsley
Salt and pepper, to taste

In a medium bowl, combine the sour cream, mustards, and parsley; mix well. Season with salt and pepper. Transfer to a jar or bowl and cover tightly. May be stored in the refrigerator for up to 1 week.

In 1410, the average European
household used eighty-four pints of mustard annually.

TWO-MUSTARD GARLIC CREAM SAUCE

This rich cream sauce, spiked with two kinds of mustard, is delicious drizzled over poached chicken breasts and roasted pork loin, or tossed with hot cooked pasta.

Makes about 1 ½ cups.

2 cups heavy whipping cream
2 cloves garlic, minced
2 tablespoons Champagne Mustard (page 47), Tarragon Mustard (page 29),
    or Dijon mustard
2 tablespoons Maple–Apple Cider Mustard (page 27), or British Beer Mustard
    (page 30)
White pepper, to taste

Place the cream and garlic in a large sauté pan. Bring to a boil over high heat, stirring constantly. Cook for 7 to 8 minutes, stirring constantly to prevent the mixture from boiling over, until the mixture is thick enough to coat the back of a spoon. Add the mustards and pepper and mix well. Serve immediately.

American Indians once dried mustard seeds
and used them as a flavoring agent.
They also ate the tender young shoots and flowers
of the plant.

57

CLASSIC MUSTARD VINAIGRETTE

Use this smooth, flavorful vinaigrette drizzled over a composed vegetable salad, or simply tossed with your favorite mixed greens. It also works well as a light dressing for potato or pasta salads.

Makes about ⅔ cup.

1 tablespoon Tarragon Mustard (page 29), Champagne Mustard (page 47),
    or Herbed Tomato Mustard (page 37)
1 clove garlic, minced
½ cup extra-virgin olive oil
2 tablespoons red wine vinegar
2 teaspoons minced fresh tarragon, or 1 teaspoon dried tarragon
Salt and pepper, to taste

Place the mustard, garlic, and olive oil in a medium bowl. Slowly add the vinegar, whisking constantly to make a smooth emulsion. Add the tarragon, season with salt and pepper, and mix well. Store in a tightly covered container in the refrigerator for up to 1 week.

Two-Mustard Mayonnaise

Classic aioli is made with just one mustard and plenty of garlic, but this version, made with two kinds of mustard, is more flavorful, making it ideal for serving with cooked vegetables, seafood, poultry, and meats, or for use as a sandwich spread.

Makes about 1 cup.

1 tablespoon Three-Citrus Mustard (page 51), or Hot Chili Coarse-Grained
　　Mustard (page 36)
1 tablespoon Tarragon Mustard (page 29), Champagne Mustard (page 47),
　　or Dijon mustard
1 clove garlic, minced
2 egg yolks
½ teaspoon salt
½ cup vegetable oil
½ cup olive oil
1 tablespoon champagne vinegar or white wine vinegar
Black pepper, to taste

Place the mustards, garlic, egg yolks, and salt in a medium bowl; mix well. Slowly add the vegetable oil, one drop at a time, whisking constantly until a smooth emulsion starts to form. When all of the vegetable oil has been added, add the olive oil in a thin stream, whisking constantly to make a smooth emulsion. Add the vinegar and season with black pepper to taste. The mayonnaise may be stored in a tightly covered container in the refrigerator for 2 weeks.

MUSTARD-PICKLED ORANGES AND LIMES

This Indian condiment is ideal for true lovers of mustard. Hot and spicy from both chili peppers and mustard, these tart orange and lime wedges are best served with rich, coconut-based stews, intensely flavored curries, and grain dishes. Shake well and drain slightly before serving the pickles.

Makes about 3 cups pickled fruit.

½ cup whole brown mustard seeds, coarsely ground
4 small dried red Chinese or Mexican chili peppers, coarsely chopped
4 small juice oranges, washed and cut into eighths
4 limes, washed and cut into eighths
1 quart water
½ cup kosher salt
½ cup mustard powder

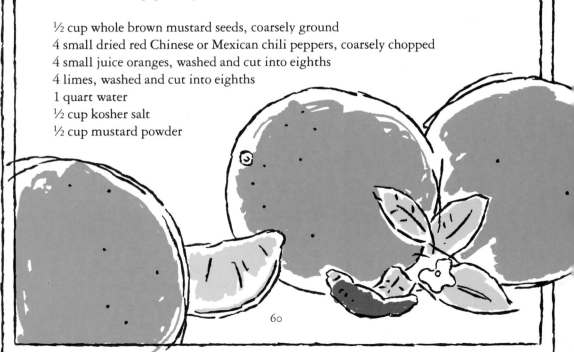

Place the mustard seeds, chili peppers, oranges, and limes in a large bowl. Bring the water and salt to boil in a large saucepan. When the water has come to a boil, pour it over the fruit and mustard seeds. Mix well and cool to room temperature.

Place the mustard powder in a small bowl. Add ½ cup of the cooled cooking liquid and mix to form a paste. Add to the fruit and mix well. Transfer to a large jar or container and cover tightly. Refrigerate for at least 2 weeks before using. Will keep in the refrigerator for up to 4 weeks after it has cured.

THREE-MUSTARD DRESSING

This mustard dressing is terrific tossed with cooked new potatoes and green beans, or com-bined with cooked and cooled pasta and chunks of smoked meat such as ham, turkey, or chicken. This dressing is also delicious made with Hazelnut Mustard (page 28) and Maple–Apple Cider Mustard (page 27), or Five-Spice Brown Mustard (page 32) and Molasses Mustard (page 45).

Makes about 1 1/4 cups.

2 tablespoons Dijon mustard
1 tablespoon German-Style Coarse-Grained Mustard (page 40)
1 tablespoon Honey Mustard (page 34)
2 tablespoons sherry wine vinegar
¾ cup olive oil
Zest from 1 lemon
2 cloves garlic, minced
Salt and pepper, to taste

Place the mustards and vinegar in a medium bowl; mix well. Slowly add the olive oil, whisking constantly to form a smooth emulsion. Add the lemon zest, garlic, salt, and pepper. The dressing may be stored in a tightly covered con-tainer in the refrigerator for up to 1 week.

HONEY MUSTARD MARINADE

Ideal for chicken or pork, this slightly sweet, sticky marinade is especially good with chicken wings. Marinate the wings in the marinade overnight, then grill them on the barbecue the next day. Alternatively, roast the wings in a large roasting pan in the oven at 400°F for about 15 minutes.

Makes about 2 cups.

½ cup Honey Mustard (page 34)
½ cup peanut oil
¼ cup lemon juice
¼ cup soy sauce
¼ cup ground sesame seeds
2 teaspoons crushed red chili pepper flakes
3 cloves garlic, minced
2 teaspoons finely ground black pepper

Place the mustard in a large bowl. Slowly add the oil, whisking constantly with a wire whisk to form a smooth emulsion. Slowly add the lemon juice and soy sauce, whisking constantly. Add the sesame seeds, red chili pepper flakes, garlic, and black pepper and mix well. The marinade may be stored in a tightly covered container in the refrigerator for up to 2 weeks.

MOSTARDA DI CREMONA — ITALIAN PRESERVED FRUITS

This unusual northern Italian condiment is traditionally served as an accompaniment to roasted wild game and poultry. Original versions contained orange and lemon peel and black mustard seed, but contemporary versions are made with a mixture of fresh and dried fruits, such as figs, plums, apricots, pumpkin or squash, and melon, mixed with mustard seed oil and a sweet syrup. Since mustard seed oil is difficult to find, I have re-created this savory-sweet condiment using mustard seeds and powder.

Makes about 2 1/2 cups.

2 cups water
2 cups sugar
1/4 cup whole yellow mustard seeds, finely ground
1/4 cup mustard powder
1 small apple, peeled, cored, and cut into six pieces
1 small pear, peeled, cored, and cut into quarters
2 rounds dried pineapple, cut into quarters
8 dried figs, stemmed and halved
2 firm apricots, pitted and quartered
1 teaspoon salt

Place the water, sugar, mustard seeds, and powder in a 10-quart heavy-bottomed saucepan. Bring to a boil over high heat, stirring frequently. Boil for 10 to 12 minutes or until the liquid is thick and syrupy. Remove from the heat.

Cook the apple and pear in boiling water to cover for 3 to 4 minutes or until tender. Drain well and add to the syrup along with the pineapple, figs, apricots, and salt; mix well and cool to room temperature. Transfer to a container, cover, and refrigerate for at least 2 weeks before serving. Will keep for several months in the refrigerator.

HERBED TOMATO MUSTARD–CORNBREAD STUFFING

Laced with the essence of prepared mustard, this satisfying stuffing is spiked with whole seeds that add an additional layer of flavor as well as a pleasing texture. Delicious eaten straight from the pan, it's also good for stuffing poultry, a leg of lamb, or a pork roast.

Makes about 4 cups.

1 large onion, cut into small dice
2 ribs celery, cut into small dice
3 cloves garlic, minced
¼ cup peanut oil
3 tablespoons whole brown mustard seeds
2 cups chicken stock or low-salt chicken broth
4 cups packaged cornbread stuffing
2 tablespoons Herbed Tomato Mustard (page 37), Maple–Apple Cider Mustard
   (page 27), or Five-Spice Brown Mustard (page 32)
Salt and pepper, to taste

In a large sauté pan, sauté the onion, celery, and garlic in the peanut oil over high heat for 5 minutes, stirring frequently. Add the mustard seeds and cook for 3 minutes. Add the chicken stock and cornbread stuffing; mix well. Cook over high heat for 2 minutes, without stirring, or until the bottom is browned.

Stir the stuffing, turning the browned bottom layer to the top and the unbrowned stuffing to the bottom. Cook for an additional 2 to 3 minutes or until the bottom is browned.

Remove from the heat, stir in the mustard, and season with salt and pepper. Serve hot, or cool to room temperature before using as a stuffing for poultry or meat. The stuffing may be stored in a tightly covered container in the refrigerator for up to 3 days. Bring to room temperature before using as a stuffing.

Some vitamin companies use mustard seed powder in combination with other natural ingredients as an appetite suppressant and metabolism elevator.

MUSTARD AND DARK BEER MARINADE

Hot, sweet, and assertive, this is an excellent marinade for beef, pork, or lamb. The mustard and mustard powder add flavor and texture, the oil coats the meat—priming it for grilling or roasting—and the beer acts as a flavoring agent and tenderizer.

Makes about 3 cups.

½ cup Molasses Mustard (page 45), Five-Spice Brown Mustard (page 32),
    or British Beer Mustard (page 30)
¼ cup mustard powder
½ cup honey
½ cup peanut oil
1 cup dark beer or ale
2 teaspoons each ground fennel seeds, caraway seeds, and black pepper
2 cloves garlic, minced

Place the mustard, mustard powder, and honey in a large bowl; mix well. Slowly add the olive oil, whisking constantly to form a smooth emulsion. Slowly add the beer, whisking constantly. Add the spices and garlic and mix well. The marinade may be stored in a tightly covered container in the refrigerator for up to 2 weeks.

ORANGE AND BROWN SUGAR–SHERRY MUSTARD MARINADE

This fruity marinade is excellent for tenderizing and flavoring pork, lamb, or poultry. I suggest marinating meat or poultry overnight for the best results. You can also use it to baste a chicken or pork roast, but be sure to leave some water in the roasting pan so the drippings don't burn on the bottom of the pan, filling your oven with smoke!

Makes about 1 ½ cups.

½ cup Brown Sugar–Sherry Mustard (page 33)
1 tablespoon ground coriander
Zest from 1 orange
¾ cup olive oil
½ cup orange juice

Place the mustard, coriander, and orange zest in a medium bowl; mix well. Slowly add the olive oil in a thin stream, whisking constantly to form a smooth emulsion. Slowly add the orange juice, whisking constantly. Marinade may be stored in a tightly covered container in the refrigerator for up to 3 weeks.

INDEX

In the first century A.D., the Roman writer
Pliny noted mustard "has so pungent a flavor that it
burns like fire." He also listed forty remedies based on
mustard for various physical ailments.

Mustard, when combined with wine,
beer, citrus juices, peanut or olive oil, makes a
delicious basting medium for grilled meats
and poultry. To make a basting
concoction, combine ½ cup of the mustard
of your choice with ½ cup of peanut or olive oil
and ⅓ cup of white or red wine,
beer, or fresh lemon, lime, or orange juice.
One or two cloves of crushed garlic and a couple
tablespoons of fresh herbs or spices
also improves the flavor.
Mix well, and brush or spoon over meat or
poultry as it cooks on the grill.